Unpack Your Heart

7 Steps To Rewriting Your Love Story

Unpack Your Heart

7 Steps To Rewriting Your Love Story

RITA CARTER

Unpack Your Heart
7 Steps To Rewriting Your Love Story

HOV Publishing is a division of HOV, LLC.
email: hopeofvision@gmail.com
www.hovpub.com

Front Cover Design by
Inside layout by HOV Design Solutions
Editing: Valorie Wright for Genesis Literary Indulgence Editing Services LLC

ISBN Paperback: 978-1-955107-30-3
ISBN PB Journal: 978-1-955107-29-7
ISBN eBook: 978-1-955107-28-0

Printed in the United States of America

DEDICATION

I am so grateful to my Heavenly Father for giving me the passion to help others find their purpose, live authentically, and build healthy relationships, starting with Him. Thank you for your endless grace and guidance. Your love and wisdom have been my rock, guiding me every step of the way. I didn't understand why certain things happened at the time, but now I see the purpose behind it all. Turning pain into purpose has brought me immense joy, and it's a purpose I am determined to fulfill. Thank you for molding me into the woman I am today, with the confidence and determination to help others. I am honored to be a vessel for uplifting Your kingdom.

To all the courageous women who dare to unpack their hearts and rewrite their love stories, thank you. To my incredible clients at Breakthrough, your strength and resilience inspire me every day. Your journeys have profoundly shaped the insights in these pages. To my accountability partners, your honest feedback and unwavering belief in my vision have been invaluable. To my family and friends, your constant support and encouragement have been a beacon of light in my life.

To my two beautiful daughters, Cayla and Camille, who inspire me to live authentically and love deeply. I do this for you. You are my greatest joy, and your presence motivates me to be the best version of myself every day. It's my purpose to pour into you so that you are whole and complete with an intimate relationship with God.

Finally, to my loving husband, Chris, whose partnership and unwavering support over the past 18 years have been my greatest source of strength. Our journey together has taught me the true essence of love, forgiveness, and commitment.

And to every woman who picks up this book: You are brave, you are strong, and you are worthy of the love you seek. This book is a testament to your journey and a guide to help you find your true self and create the relationships you desire. Your willingness to grow, heal, and embrace change is an inspiration. May you find the courage to unpack your heart and rewrite your love story with confidence and joy.

This book is for you. May it be a companion on your journey to discovering your true worth and the boundless love that awaits you.

"Tilling the soil of a garden and rebuilding a relationship share common elements of care, effort, and nurturing. Just as tilling prepares the ground for growth, rebuilding a relationship requires cultivating an environment conducive to healing and understanding. Both processes involve breaking down barriers, removing obstacles, and creating a fertile foundation for growth."

~ Rita Carter

Unpack Your Heart

CONTENTS

Unpack Your Heart

PREFACE

When I first started Breakthrough, my mission was clear: to help women find their purpose, live authentically, and create thriving relationships. Over the years, I have had the honor of working with countless women who have faced challenges in their relationships, whether in their marriages, with significant others, or as they embarked on new romantic journeys. What I have learned from these incredible women has deeply influenced the creation of *Unpack Your Heart:*

Seven Steps to Rewriting Your Love Story.

This book is the culmination of my experiences, insights, and the transformative processes I have developed through my coaching practice. Each step outlined in this guide is designed to help you navigate the complex emotional landscape of relationships with clarity, compassion, and courage. These steps are not theoretical concepts; they are practical, actionable strategies that have proven effective time and again.

1. **Willingness & Prayer**: Embrace the power of openness and spiritual guidance as you prepare for change.

2. **Accountability & Communication**: Cultivate honesty and responsibility to build stronger, clearer connections.

3. **Forgiveness**: Heal past wounds and learn the art of letting go to move forward.

4. **Trust, Intimacy, & Vulnerability**: Develop deeper bonds by embracing trust and vulnerability.

5. **Building on a Solid Foundation**: Create a stable and supportive base for your relationship.

6. **Setting Boundaries**: Understand the importance of boundaries and how to implement them effectively.

7. **Rediscover & Adventure**: Reignite the excitement in your relationship by exploring new experiences together.

In writing this book, my goal was to provide you with a roadmap to not only rebuild and strengthen your relationships but also to rediscover yourself in the process. Each chapter is filled with practical exercises, real-life examples, and heartfelt advice to guide you through the journey of transformation.

I believe that every woman has the capacity to create the love story she desires. It starts with a willingness to look within, to embrace change, and to take intentional steps toward growth. My hope is that *Unpack Your Heart* will be a source of inspiration, guidance, and empowerment for you.

Thank you for allowing me to be a part of your journey. As you embark on this path, know that you are not alone. I am here with you, cheering you on every step of the way.

With love and gratitude,

Rita Carter

Unpack Your Heart

INTRODUCTION

Views on marriage in 2024 reflect a diverse range of perspectives, with individuals and couples navigating the complexities of modern relationships while seeking fulfillment, companionship, and stability in their personal lives. There is a growing trend of delaying marriage until later in life, with individuals focusing on education, career development, and personal growth before committing to marriage. This delay allows people to establish themselves professionally and emotionally before entering into a lifelong partnership. The fear of divorce often looms over the idea of marriage as well. I didn't have a positive model of a strong, healthy marriage. I witnessed firsthand conflicts, financial struggles, infidelity, and various forms of abuse. These experiences can instill a reluctance towards marriage, fostering a fear of committing to someone for the long haul.

Many leap into relationships or marriage for reasons that don't align with genuine connection. Baggage unknowingly tags along, clouding our path. That's why, as we navigate relationships, pondering the foundation becomes vital. It's more than the glitz of a wedding or proudly saying, "I'm married." It's about understanding the essence of a healthy bond, diving into what truly nurtures a thriving relationship. Embrace the gravity of building a healthy, fulfilling connection—it's the heartbeat of lasting love.

When was the last time you've been in or saw a healthy relationship? As a young girl, I held a steadfast dream of marriage close to my heart. Yet, reality differed; I lacked a genuine model of a thriving union. It taught me a crucial lesson: assessing your relationship is pivotal. It's about gazing at your partnership honestly—taking in its entirety. Relationships demand work and flexibility, but they should also echo your values and nurture your well-being. Take that introspective dive, ensuring the dynamic resonates with health and fulfillment.

In a world filled with picture-perfect snapshots of love, where filters embellish every moment and made-up fairytales dictate our expectations, it's easy to lose sight of the raw, unscripted reality of our own love stories. We're bombarded with narratives of 'happily ever after,' but rarely do we see the messy drafts, the crossed-out paragraphs, and the scribbled edits that shape the true chronicles of our relationships.

Whether you're newly married, weathered years together, or simply yearning for a love story of your own, welcome to a space that strips away the veneer of perfection and embraces the beautiful chaos that is love.

This isn't a book about flawless romances or enchanted castles. No, this is a roadmap for the modern woman navigating the intricate maze of relationships. It's about rewriting the narratives we've inherited, shredding the unrealistic expectations, and crafting a story that's uniquely yours—one woven with authenticity, resilience, and growth.

From the whirlwind of wedding vows to the silent battles fought behind closed doors, this book ventures into the depths of what it means to love and be loved in an era where 'forever' isn't always neatly packaged. It's a guide that doesn't promise a fairytale ending but empowers you to build a love story sturdy enough to weather life's storms.

Here, we'll explore into the unspoken struggles, the whispered fears, and the shimmering hopes that echo in the hearts of women navigating the intricate dance of companionship. Expect no magic wands or quick fixes, for love isn't about perfect formulas—it's about embracing imperfection and finding beauty in the journey.

Imagine love as a garden. It requires attention, care, and nurturing to flourish. Sometimes, weeds of doubt and resentment sprout, and they need to be addressed with patience and understanding. This book is your gardening tool, helping you tend to your relationship, ensuring it grows strong and beautiful. But let's take it a step further. Ask yourself: what does a thriving relationship look like to you? Is it about constant communication, mutual respect, shared dreams, or perhaps the simple joy of companionship? It's easy to get lost in societal definitions of what love should be. Yet, the most fulfilling relationships are those defined by the individuals within them, tailored to their unique needs and desires.

Consider this: in the vast landscape of love, there's no one-size-fits-all. Your journey might not look like your parents', your friends', or the glossy portrayals in movies. And that's okay. In fact, that's wonderful. It means your love story is truly yours, a custom-made narrative that reflects your deepest values and aspirations. As you turn these pages, reflect on your own story. Where have you been? Where do you want to go? What chapters do you wish to rewrite? This book isn't just about offering advice; it's about empowering you to take ownership of your love life. To be brave enough to confront the painful chapters, to celebrate the joyful ones, and to craft a future filled with hope and possibility.

Think about the moments that have defined your relationship. The laughter shared over inside jokes, the quiet strength during hard times, the times you've held each other up when the world seemed to fall apart. These moments, both big and small, are the true essence of love. They are the building blocks of a connection that can withstand the test of time.

Let's also consider the importance of self-love. Before you can fully love someone else, you need to love yourself. This journey is as much about understanding and valuing your own worth as it is about finding someone to share your life with. Embrace your individuality, your strengths, and your imperfections. When you bring a whole, self-aware person into a relationship, you build a foundation that is incredibly strong and resilient.

So, whether you're flipping through these pages in search of solace, seeking guidance, or simply curious about the untold chapters of your story, know that you hold within your hands a compass to navigate the complexities of modern love.

Let's embark together on a journey to rewrite your love story—a story told with authenticity, resilience, and an unwavering belief that the pen to your narrative lies firmly in your grasp. You hold the power to transform the pages of your love story into something extraordinary. With each turn of the page, you will uncover the steps to breathe new life into your relationship and create a narrative that captures hearts and leaves a lasting impression.

Are you ready to redefine love on your terms? Let's begin.

CHAPTER
ONE
BETTER is COMING

In relationships, there are two important things that can really make a difference: being open to change and praying about it. We'll focus on the importance of being willing to change and the role of prayer in building healthier, more fulfilling relationships. In the ups and downs of love, it's easy to feel overwhelmed. But this chapter is here to remind you that with an open heart and a willing spirit, better days are on the horizon. Willingness and prayer aren't just empty words; they have the power to change our love stories. Love isn't something that stays the same forever; it grows and changes. To have a strong and lasting connection, you need to be willing to change and adapt. That means being open to new things and letting go of stubbornness.

Willingness helps us face challenges and grow stronger together. It's about being brave enough to admit we don't know everything and being humble enough to learn and grow. In marriage, and in the search for it, being willing to listen, adapt, and compromise is what holds everything together. It's like a silent promise to stand by each other through thick and thin, and to celebrate together when things go well. Willingness is the starting point for any real change. It's about being ready to try new things, let go of old habits, and step into new possibilities with hope and courage. Think of willingness as the key that opens the door to a better relationship. Without it, we stay stuck in the same old patterns of hurt and disappointment. What does it mean to be truly willing? It means showing up, even when it's hard. It means saying "yes" to difficult conversations, counseling sessions, and moments of self-reflection. It means being open to new ideas and believing that better is on the way.

I yearned for change. I craved something more for my marriage. Having spent years in matrimony, raising two kids, and navigating the challenges we faced, it became an uphill battle. The stagnation weighed heavily on me. We'd weathered so many storms, yet I couldn't see how we'd evolve beyond them. It felt like we were rooted in a place of struggle, unsure of how to move forward from our shared history.

In that space, trust was absent, vulnerability was a foreign concept, and genuine peace escaped us. I sensed this lack deeply. Yet, within that realization, a longing for transformation emerged. I yearned to actively contribute to that change, to break away from the patterns I'd observed. So, I turned to prayer. I grappled with the idea of committing my life to this man. I wanted to, but the path forward remained uncertain to me. I never had a genuine model of a strong, healthy relationship, especially one that navigates the depths alongside a spouse through significant highs and lows. Betrayals, trust fractures, and the weight of baggage—be it from childhood experiences or past relationships—all shadowed our marriage. The question lingered: How do I evolve beyond these challenges?

Like many, I found my thoughts spiraling into negativity, cluttering my mind with distractions. Feeling trapped within a relationship creates a daunting challenge, yet I believed there had to be an escape from that stagnation—a path towards positive transformation. It was crucial for me to pause, to introspect on why I felt confined within my marriage. I sought to uncover the underlying reasons, understanding that clarity and insight were essential for change. I opened myself to vulnerability, ready to embrace a different approach. As I embraced willingness, I had to remember the wisdom of Philippians 4:13: "I can do all things through Christ who strengthens me." This scripture reminded me that I am not alone in our efforts. With faith and willingness, I had the strength to face challenges and embrace change.

Prayer is a powerful tool in building a strong relationship. Prayer isn't just petitions of words uttered in hope; it's a beacon of intention and reflection. It's the art of carving out sacred moments to connect with God, seeking guidance, solace, and gratitude. Prayer in relationships isn't about pleading to God to alter the will of another but rather a practice that aligns our intentions, centers our hearts, and fills our actions with purpose. It's about seeking clarity, wisdom, and the strength to navigate the ebb and flow of love's journey. In the purity of prayer, we don't ask for flawless relationships, for that's an unattainable fantasy. Instead, we pray for the wisdom to understand, the patience to endure, and the grace to accept both ourselves and our partners in their entirety.

I found myself turning to Jeremiah 29:11 - "For I know the plans I have for you," declares the Lord, "plans to prosper you and not to harm you, plans to give you hope and a future" as I started my journey. We both knew we needed to change and we wanted to but how? Prayer also involves letting go. It's about recognizing that some things are beyond our control and trusting God to guide you. It reminds us that we are not alone in our struggles, and with faith and patience, better days are ahead. Also, consider Matthew 21:22: "And whatever you ask in prayer, you will receive, if you have faith." This scripture highlights the power of prayer and faith in manifesting positive changes in your relationship.

When willingness and prayer link, a powerful transformation transpires—one that nurtures the soil in which love flourishes. It's about aligning our desires with our actions, infusing our relationships with intention, and surrendering to God's will that guides our paths. Together, they create a strong force for change. Willingness opens the door, and prayer gives you the strength and guidance to walk through it.

By fostering a heart willing to bend, learn, and adapt, and by embracing prayer as a compass guiding our intentions, we invite transformation into our love stories. It's not a swift conversion but a gradual unfolding, a continuous journey towards a deeper understanding of ourselves and our partners.

I examined my current situation to envision the future I desired—not a continuation of the present. Recognizing the need for change, I understood it wouldn't come without discomfort. However, the crucial aspect was our mutual commitment to this journey. It required both of us to embrace vulnerability and step into the unknown together, even when it felt uncomfortable. Two willing individuals, ready to navigate discomfort for the sake of something different and better. We needed to embrace discomfort, to willingly delve into heart and soul searching. There was a necessity to reflect deeply, to discern how we arrived at this place. Our relationship was nowhere near perfect, but we were determined to have a fresh start. When my husband and I began our marital journey, it was adorned with beauty, dreams, and aspirations. Our wedding was a cherished memory, and our achievements—education, homes—seemed like milestones. Yet, in the middle of this apparent success, we questioned the strength of our foundation.

Reflecting on it, I can honestly admit that our foundation wasn't solid. To be completely frank, we weren't adequately prepared for marriage. We were young and in the midst of discovering our individual identities, yet we chose to marry despite that. As time passed, we got into the habit of hiding our problems, but eventually, we discovered that the problems we avoided addressing started causing us to stumble. The challenges in our relationships became so noticeable that navigating it became dangerous and unhealthy. Thankfully, we managed to grow together because both of us were committed to doing the work. We were ready to put in the effort. Was it simple? Not at all. But our willingness to put in the work made the difference. Now, if you're still in the process of healing from past trauma, whether it's from childhood or previous relationships, this book might not be the immediate solution for you. If you feel that you have done the work, this can be a guide to starting a relationship the right way to avoid some of the obstacles that people like myself experienced. It's crucial to seek self-help and heal from those experiences before exploring this journey of love. This became a vital part of my quest for a healthy, strong relationship. Unknowingly, both my husband and I carried baggage into our marriage. We entered our union burdened by these unresolved issues. I strongly urge you to seek individual help, to confront and address your personal baggage, to achieve wholeness and healing. This prepares you to embark on the journey of rewriting your love story with a stronger foundation.

The journey to rewrite your love story begins within yourself. It's essential to prioritize your own well-being first. A healthy, complete relationship stems from your individual wholeness. Concentrate on your personal growth, embrace self-compassion, and acknowledge your resilience. Discover activities and passions that bring you joy independently of the relationship. Dedicate time to self-care, nurture your interests, and cultivate a strong self-identity. Remember, within you lies the strength to progress, fostering a renewed sense of self-worth. Many tend to bury their emotions—I certainly did. Some carry unresolved trauma and negative emotions from their past. It's crucial to address these issues. Take proactive steps, seek guidance, consult a counselor, and allow yourself to be vulnerable. Identify the areas where healing is necessary. In my case, healing was needed in relation to my absent father. Identifying these pivotal points is essential for your personal growth and healing journey. Though my father was physically present at home, he remained emotionally distant. This lack of emotional connection lingered within me for years, impacting my decisions. I made choices that weren't right for me, enduring hurt and entering relationships I shouldn't have. The pain stemming from this absence of an emotional bond with my father affected my choices and relationships significantly.

I began witnessing and experiencing things that compounded my existing trauma, and regrettably, I carried that burden into my marriage. The weight of not feeling genuinely loved stayed with me. I realized I needed to embark on personal healing. Before being open with my husband, I had to first confront my vulnerabilities alone. To rewrite your love story, it's crucial to embark on a personal journey, unraveling the complexities of your heart. Remember, everyone's healing timeline varies, so give yourself grace as you navigate this process. Respecting my husband's journey, allowing him space to heal and accepting him for who he is as a man became essential.

Often, modern marriages are founded on glamour, but when we say "I do," it's not just to the person on that day; it's a commitment to the person they'll become. It's often overlooked. With growth and time, there might come a moment when you look at your partner and wonder, "Who are you now?" It's not the same person I married, not the one I envisioned spending my life with. It's highly likely there are hidden layers you have yet uncovered. That's why embracing vulnerability is crucial. Be open with yourself, accepting where you are on your journey thus far. This vulnerability enables personal growth, allowing you to evolve into the person destined for your path. Only by becoming the person you're meant to be can you lay the foundation for a healthy and thriving relationship with your significant other.

If you're already in a place of wholeness and healing, that's wonderful. However, for many of us who entered marriage without being fully healed, there's hope. It's never too late to rewrite your story. Seeking guidance from a coach—an impartial individual—can offer valuable insights, tools, and techniques to navigate challenges, enhance communication, and discover new paths forward. Embrace the belief that better days lie ahead. It's about being willing to step forward into that desired future state. It's not solely about where you are now but the direction you're aiming for. Take a moment to reflect on your aspirations.

Consider where you and your partner currently stand and how your journeys have led you here. Pose this crucial question to yourself: Can I envision a lifetime with this person? If your answer is yes, it's a significant first step. However, before anything else, you must engage in individual work. Begin there, commit to the process, and through personal growth, you'll pave the way to building the foundation that should have been present when you both said, "I do."

We frequently encounter numerous reasons why people might choose not to enter or remain in marriage. However, there's a wealth of rewards woven into the fabric of a healthy relationship. Imagine this: Love doesn't just affect individuals; it spreads to families and echoes throughout society. Think about how it fills our lives with emotions, making us happier and healthier. Love is like a strong foundation for physical health and keeping families together, creating a home where everyone feels safe and cared for. And when it comes to mental health, being surrounded by love can heal deep wounds. Plus, there are financial benefits too! When couples talk openly about finances, it brings stability and empowerment. And let's not forget about the social side of love—it connects us with others, offering support when times are tough and building bonds with other couples who are on a similar journey. These glimpses are just the beginning of the vast benefits awaiting those committed to building a robust, thriving marriage. Trust me, the effort is worth every moment invested in crafting that foundation.

Below are some exercises that I used to help me apply willingness and prayer on the journey of rewriting my love story:

WILLINGNESS:

1. **Journal**: Think about areas in your relationship where you feel stuck. Write down your thoughts and set small, achievable goals.

   What are you willing to change?

   ____

   ____

   ____

   What fears do you need to face?

   ____

   ____

   ____

   ____

2. **Daily Affirmations**: Start each day with affirmations that remind you to stay open to change. For example, "I am open to new possibilities," or "I am willing to work towards a healthier relationship."

   ____

---

3. **Action Plan**: Make a plan for dealing with specific issues in your relationship. Identify steps you're willing to take and commit to them, like seeking counseling, improving communication, or spending more quality time together.

PRAYER:

1. **Gratitude Prayer**: Begin and end each day with a prayer of gratitude. Focus on the good things in your relationship and express thanks for your partner and the love you share.

---

2. **Meditative Prayer**: Set aside time each day for quiet, meditative prayer. Find a peaceful spot, close your eyes, and focus on your breath. Use this time to connect with your inner self and seek guidance for your relationship.

____

____

3. **Praying for Your Relationship**: Pray specifically for your relationship and your partner. Ask for strength, patience, and wisdom to handle challenges. Trust that your prayers will be heard and that better days are coming.

____

____

____

TAKE ACTION:

1. How can changing how you look at your past relationships, from wishing for what's gone to hoping for what's ahead, change how you try to make your love life better by being open and praying?

____

____

____

2. How does the idea that "Better is Coming" make you rethink how you see love? Does it push you to actively work towards making your love life better, rather than just waiting for fate to take its course?

____

____

____

Notes:

CHAPTER
TWO

BRINGING LIGHT to DARK PLACES

What's been **YOUR** roadblock? You've put in the effort on yourself, seeking help to address past traumas unrelated to your partner. You've undergone the necessary work, healing from past relationship wounds and personal struggles. Now, you're equipped to step ahead confidently in your current relationship. Well done on your progress! What's causing a halt in this relationship? Do you feel trapped, unable to progress? Could it be trust issues, stemming from past betrayals, hindering your steps forward? Or perhaps a lack of intimacy? Is communication posing a barrier? Embracing discomfort might be the key to unlocking these obstacles.

I had to face the truth: I married someone who wasn't prepared, and that realization stung. Truth be told, I wasn't fully prepared either. There are two crucial elements of a healthy relationship: accountability and communication. Every relationship faces challenges, but with the right tools, you can bring light to these dark places and create a deeper connection with your partner.

Accountability means taking responsibility for your actions, words, and feelings. It's about admitting your mistakes, owning up to your part in any conflicts, and being honest with yourself and your partner. Think of your relationship as a house. Accountability is like the strong framework that holds the house together. Without it, the house becomes unstable. By being accountable, you keep your relationship strong and steady. Embrace accountability for the role you played in your relationship journey. There might have been early signs or concerns that you chose to overlook—those moments of hesitation or uncertainty. It's time to acknowledge where you stand without shifting the blame solely onto your partner.

Accountability is a powerful ingredient in rewriting your love story, infusing it with integrity, trust, and personal growth. When you willingly take responsibility, you exhibit transparency and authenticity in your interactions. It involves holding yourself accountable for the impact of your words and actions, addressing mistakes with humility and honesty. This ownership fosters a culture of trust and respect, vital elements for the flourishing of your relationship.

Now, it's time to face the music and hold yourself accountable for those red flags you chose to overlook. Taking responsibility isn't a heavy load to carry; it shows how strong and honest we are in a relationship. It means being ready to admit when we've done something wrong or when things aren't going well in our partnership. Admitting our faults, actions, and feelings isn't a sign of being weak; it shows how dedicated we are to getting better. Within the context of love, accountability paves the way for authentic connections. It's the cornerstone upon which trust, respect, and understanding grows. When we take responsibility for our words and actions, we build bridges instead of creating walls, fostering an environment where honesty and vulnerability can thrive. We breakthrough the barriers to communication, fostering an environment where transparency can exist.

Accountability is a shared duty between partners. Both taking responsibility contributes to the relationship's growth and overall well-being. Integrating accountability into your love story lays the groundwork for a narrative rooted in understanding. There might be moments where you notice red flags or hear things that make you uncertain—I've been there. Despite those reservations, I chose to marry and I knew we weren't prepared. Taking accountability for your actions is crucial. If I had addressed my concerns early on, perhaps our journey would have taken a different course.

But the sheer excitement of youthful love and the belief in a perfect marriage doesn’t shield you from reality. It simply doesn’t. To truly forgive my husband, I had to acknowledge my part in our relationship. I was striving excessively to be the ideal wife, losing myself in the process. I was so fixated on being the perfect spouse that I neglected my own needs and overlooked warning signs along the way. I brushed aside certain concerns that bothered me, even though I eventually married him. Clear and sincere communication is vital in understanding each other's needs, desires, and worries. It's the gateway to resolving problems effectively, expressing emotions, and fostering a profound emotional bond. Enhancing communication enables you to confront past issues, voice your dreams, and shape a collective vision for your shared future. It helps you see clearly, understand each other better, and work through problems together. Good communication can turn potential conflicts into opportunities for growth and deeper connection. Key aspects of effective communication include:

1. **Active Listening**: Pay full attention when your partner is speaking. Show that you value their perspective by

nodding, maintaining eye contact, and responding appropriately.

2. **Empathy**: Try to understand your partner's feelings and point of view. Empathy bridges the gap between differing perspectives and fosters compassion.

3. **Clarity**: Be clear and direct in your communication. Avoid vague statements and express your thoughts and feelings honestly.

4. **Non-Verbal Cues**: Pay attention to body language, facial expressions, and tone of voice. These can often convey more than words alone.

5. **Regular Check-Ins**: Make time for regular conversations about your relationship. Discuss what's going well, what needs improvement, and how you can support each other better.

When accountability and communication come together, it's like unlocking a door to deeper understanding and trust in relationships. It's about not only owning up to our actions and feelings but also expressing them openly and honestly. This combination creates a solid foundation for resolving conflicts, building stronger connections, and moving forward together with mutual respect and understanding. This reminds me that rewriting our love story isn't about erasing the past but rather transforming it into a space where resilience and growth resides. It's about acknowledging that relationships aren't flawless but are improved by our ability to hold ourselves accountable and to communicate in a way that our partner can understand.

Transparent communication serves as the foundation for setting boundaries. Articulating needs, worries, and boundaries openly constructs the framework for mutual understanding. In a world filled with daily distractions that breed misunderstandings, nurturing effective communication becomes crucial for navigating relationships. Effective communication occurs when you convey your message in a manner that others can comprehend. Merely speaking at length with a rich vocabulary isn't sufficient if your message is not received as intended. When communication is clear, it is no longer a barrier; instead, they transform into pathways leading partners toward mutual respect and understanding.

This phase of the journey might be challenging and uncomfortable. It could sting; it might even be painful. Yet, navigating this path is necessary to reach the other side. Confronting these areas are crucial. After being open with yourself, the next step is to dismantle those barriers and be open with your partner. It's time to embrace candid and sincere communication with your significant other, sharing how you truly feel. Apart from making God the center of our relationship, good communication is like the glue that holds everything in every successful love story. In rewriting your love story, effective communication takes on an even more pivotal role. Voice any lingering concerns, desires, and other aspects that might be contributing to a sense of stagnation in your relationship.

It's important to create a safe space for open dialogue, active listening, and understanding. This needs to be a heartfelt conversation and a judgement free zone. Addressing these concerns can pave the way for growth and progress. Remember, effective communication is not just about speaking, it's also about active listening. Truly hear your significant other's words, emotions, and unspoken desires. Show genuine curiosity, empathy, and understanding as you engage in the beautiful dance of communication. Through open and ongoing communication, you can co-create a love story that exceeds your wildest dreams.

Sit your significant other down and have an open conversation about your commitment to putting in the effort. Embrace honesty and transparency, even though it might be uncomfortable and challenging. Recognize that some discussions with your spouse or significant other may be painful, similar to addressing wounds from childhood mishaps. Remember those times when you had a scraped knee, and someone helped clean it, putting a bandage on to stop the bleeding. Now, it's like taking off that bandage—you have to expose the wound to air for true healing to begin. Yes, it might hurt, and peeling off the bandage can be tough. Perhaps it feels like wanting to rip it off quickly, just like that memorable bike incident. Acknowledge the discomfort but understand that this step is crucial for genuine healing. Just like my knee needed to heal, relationships require bringing everything to the surface so it can heal. In your journey together, reveal what's causing pain and hindering progress. What's the obstacle holding you both back? It's crucial to lay it bare, allowing the healing process to unfold. Let the wounds be exposed, and together, breathe new life into your relationship. Keep in mind that there are different ways to communicate.

I remember a time when my husband and I couldn't talk without arguing. We were always walking on eggshells to avoid conflict. Something had to change. One day, I wrote my husband a letter, and for the first time, I felt like he really understood me. That was when we started writing letters to each other, even though we lived in the same house. Writing was the only way we could be honest without fear of judgment or interruptions. It felt like we were getting to know each other again, like in a long-distance relationship. We listened not just to respond, but to truly understand each other. This new way of communicating allowed us to see each other in a new light and sparked a desire to learn more about our relationship. It was the beginning of something different and better.

Effective communication is the key to healing and achieving wholeness in your relationship. Your words reflect what's in your heart; it's a mirror to your inner world. If there's bitterness or resentment in your heart, it will manifest in your speech. Unpacking your heart, delving into its roots, and confronting what holds you back is essential. Identify what you can't release or what refuses to release you. Doing this work is a shared responsibility—both partners must be willing. Embracing discomfort, I found myself having in-depth, uncomfortable discussions with my husband. Throughout the range of emotions, navigating through the complexity, I had to dive deep and put in the necessary work.

What you say reflects the state of your heart. If bitterness, anger, and frustration reside in your hurt, it's time to unpack it. Only then can you speak words of peace, joy, love, healing, and growth. Your hurt holds you back and facing it head-on is the first step. The journey of problem solving might be painful but focus on reaching the other side. It's like running a race – sometimes your legs ache, you get a cramp, or your stomach feels queasy. Keep moving forward, even if you need to slow down or take a walk. The key is to persevere, to keep going until you reach that other side. You'll get there. You're a natural problem solver, and this challenge is within your capacity to conquer and fix. However, it demands your commitment to the work. Identify what's holding you back, shine a light on the shadows within your relationship. True prosperity and growth come when you unpack your heart and dive into the necessary work. So, roll up your sleeves and let's get to it! Remember, the journey to a better relationship is ongoing. Keep practicing accountability and effective communication, and you'll continue to see positive changes in your love story. As you move forward, let these tools guide you, bringing light and understanding to every corner of your relationship.

TAKE ACTION:

1. How can being honest about the tough issues in your relationships, and talking about it openly and kindly, help you make your love life better by taking responsibility for your actions?

   ____

   ____

   ____

2. How do you deal with the difficult and awkward parts of talking with your partner, and how can being accountable help, you see those tricky areas more clearly, so you can grow closer and make your love story stronger?

___

___

___

Notes:

CHAPTER
THREE

EMBRACING IMPERFECTIONS

Having invested time in your personal growth, tackling childhood or past relationship traumas, and emerging healed, you've bravely ventured into the work on your current relationship. The journey involved a rollercoaster of emotions—uncomfortable conversations, tears, laughter, jokes, reflections, and reminiscing. Now, everything's laid out on the table, and it's the moment to gaze at your significant other and ask yourself if moving forward is feasible. This journey is tailor-made for those who genuinely desire to progress and build a future together.

As you observed your loved one in the vulnerability of revealed truths, both of you have bared your souls, shared openly, and exposed the raw reality. Now comes the challenging part—forgiveness for what transpired. I get it; this phase was tough for me too. It meant revisiting the pain and trauma I experienced in my relationship, confronting the lingering questions, uncertainties, and the puzzling areas that didn't add up. It was about delving into that discomfort, feeling the pain, and addressing what held me back. But trust me, facing it head-on is a vital step in the journey. Forgiveness is a transformative force that plays a crucial role in rewriting your love story. It has the power to heal wounds, release burdens, and create fertile ground for new beginnings and growth. Forgiveness allows you to let go of resentment, anger, and pain, freeing you and your partner from the shackles of the past. Everyone has flaws and makes mistakes—it's part of being human. In a relationship, it's easy to focus on your partner's shortcomings and forget that you, too, have imperfections. Embracing imperfections means accepting your partner as they are, flaws and all, and recognizing that love isn't about finding someone perfect but about accepting and loving someone imperfectly.

Forgiveness isn't a grand gesture granted to others; it's a sacred gift we offer ourselves. It's the act of releasing the grip of resentment, relinquishing the chains that bind us to past hurts, and allowing the winds of healing to sweep through our souls. And through forgiveness, we release the weight of grudges, allowing space for empathy and understanding to bloom. Holding onto grudges or past mistakes creates a barrier between you and your partner. Forgiveness breaks down these barriers and opens the door to a healthier, more loving connection.

In relationships, Forgiveness isn't about forgetting the hurt like it never happened. Instead, it's like medicine for our hearts, easing the pain so we can move on and feel hopeful again. It's a conscious choice to extend grace, to embrace imperfections, and to understand that within the realm of love, mistakes are inevitable. Forgiving doesn't mean forgetting or condoning hurtful actions; rather, it is a conscious choice to release the negative emotions associated with those actions. It grants you the opportunity to move forward with a clean slate, allowing space for positive change and growth within your love story.

By practicing forgiveness, you open doors to deeper understanding and empathy. It enables you to view your partner's flaws and mistakes with compassion, recognizing their capacity for growth and evolution. Think of forgiveness as a bridge. On one side, there's hurt and resentment. On the other side, there's healing and reconciliation. Forgiveness is the bridge that helps you move from pain to peace, from conflict to harmony. Similarly, forgiveness encourages self-reflection and acceptance, allowing you to acknowledge your own shortcomings and seek personal growth. Moreover, forgiveness fosters a sense of emotional safety within your love story.

When both partners embrace forgiveness, it creates an environment where vulnerability, honesty, and open communication can thrive. It encourages the willingness to address past grievances, learn from them, and create healthier patterns of behavior moving forward.

In the process of rewriting your love story, forgiveness serves as a bridge between the past and the future. It allows you to release the weight of old wounds, nurture the present moment, and envision a future filled with love, understanding, and shared dreams. By embracing forgiveness, you can infuse your narrative with a renewed sense of hope, resilience, and the potential for a deeper, more fulfilling connection with your partner. Remember, forgiveness is a continuous practice—a choice that you make every day to let go of past grievances and choose love instead. As you rewrite your love story, allow forgiveness to be the guiding light that paves the way for a more beautiful and harmonious narrative.

My husband and I had to lay it all out, be genuinely open and vulnerable, sharing that uncharted side of our story. It hit me—the immense weight I was carrying. Forgiveness, I realized, isn't a gift to the other person; it's a liberation for yourself. I was stuck because I couldn't truly forgive. Yeah, I said the words, but my actions told a different story. Despite my verbal forgiveness, I found myself still discussing it, shedding tears, and questioning every move, every call—basically, everything under the sun. It was an inconsistency I needed to unravel. I had to take a hard look and admit that, in retrospect, I hadn't genuinely forgiven my husband or moved past our shared trauma. It hit me—I needed something more. So, I turned to prayer, desperate to salvage my marriage. It dawned on me; the forgiveness I sought from God, why couldn't I extend that to my husband? Countless times, I've made wrong choices, bad decisions, been in the wrong relationships, and surrounded myself with the wrong crowd. Yet, I'd return to God, seeking forgiveness. It made me ponder—if God can forgive someone like me, why on earth couldn't I forgive my husband?

If God is gracious enough to forgive me, why not extend that grace to him? Yet, I had to remind myself—I'm not divine; I'm human, burdened with emotions. The key was meeting him where he was. I had placed him on a pedestal, this image of perfection, and that needed to change. Realizing he's human, on a journey to betterment with his fair share of mistakes, shattered my idealized view. Does he deserve forgiveness? Absolutely. The challenge was in finding a way to forgive him and forge ahead.

The next step on my journey to true forgiveness was a revelation. I had to confront my own actions and take accountability. Now, this doesn't mean I pushed my husband to betray me. What it means is acknowledging that I married him, fully aware that we weren't ready. I knew he wasn't prepared to be the husband I needed, and I wasn't ready to be the wife he deserved. We were young, clueless, and lacked examples of a healthy relationship. Despite it all, we dove headfirst into marriage, and that realization hit me like a ton of bricks.

Here's my encouragement for you: Be open to forgiveness. Holding onto resentment is like strapping a ton of weight onto your shoulders—it only burdens you. The release isn't just for your spouse or significant other; it's a gift to yourself. Now, if you find forgiveness possible but staying isn't, that's your call, your business and we have to respect that. Forgiveness doesn't mean you have to stay. But if your aim is to stay and forgive, and you're uncertain how to begin, start with prayer. Acknowledge your imperfections and the human journey you're both navigating. Remember, forgiveness is a journey, not a one-time event. It requires patience, understanding, and a commitment to letting go of past hurts. By embracing forgiveness, you can bring light to the dark places in your relationship and pave the way for a more loving and fulfilling connection.

Forgiveness can be challenging, especially when the hurt runs deep. However, taking small steps can make the process more manageable. Here are a few to consider:

1. **Acknowledge Your Pain**: It's important to recognize and accept your feelings. Ignoring your pain won't make it go away. Talk about your feelings with your partner or a trusted friend to help process them.

   ____
   ____
   ____

2. **Understand the Impact**: Reflect on how holding onto anger and resentment is affecting your relationship and your well-being. Realize that forgiveness is as much for your own peace as it is for your partner.

   ____
   ____
   ____

3. **Communicate Openly**: Have an honest conversation with your partner about what hurt you. Use "I" statements to express your feelings without blaming or accusing.

   ____
   ____
   ____

4. **Seek Understanding**: Try to understand your partner's perspective. This doesn't mean you have to agree with them, but empathy can help you see the situation in a new light.

   ____
   ____
   ____

5. **Make a Conscious Decision**: Decide to forgive. Forgiveness is a choice, and making that choice can be empowering. It doesn't mean the hurt will disappear immediately, but it sets you on the path to healing.

   ____
   ____
   ____
   ____

6. **Let Go of Resentment**: Holding onto resentment only hurts you in the long run. Practice letting go, even if it's a little bit at a time. This might involve redirecting your thoughts or finding healthy outlets for your emotions.

   ____
   ____
   ____

7. **Move Forward Together**: After forgiving, focus on rebuilding trust and strengthening your connection. Use

the experience as a lesson and an opportunity to grow together.

____
____
____

PRACTICAL EXERCISES:

1. **Forgiveness Letter**: Write a letter to your partner (you don't have to give it to them) where you express your hurt and explain why you're choosing to forgive. This can help you articulate your feelings and start the healing process.

   ____
   ____
   ____

2. **Reflection Journal**: Keep a journal where you reflect on times you've forgiven someone and how it made you feel. Also, note instances when you've been forgiven and how it impacted you. This can reinforce the value of forgiveness.

   ____
   ____
   ____

3. **Daily Affirmations**: Use daily affirmations to remind yourself of the power of forgiveness. Phrases like "I

choose to forgive and let go" can help reinforce a forgiving mindset.

4. **Forgiveness Ritual**: Create a ritual to symbolize letting go of past hurts. This could be as simple as writing down your grievances and then tearing up the paper or burning it as a way of releasing the negative energy.

TAKE ACTION:

1. How does the act of forgiveness reshape your love story, transforming past wounds into opportunities for growth and deeper connection within your relationship?

2. In what ways can embracing forgiveness allow you to break free from the chains of resentment and bitterness, paving the way for a more authentic and resilient love story filled with acceptance and grace?

Notes:

Notes:

CHAPTER FOUR

BEYOND the SURFACE

The elements of trust, intimacy, and vulnerability are the backbone of a deep and meaningful relationship. When you move beyond the surface, you find the true connection that makes your bond unbreakable. Trust is the bedrock of any relationship. Without it, doubts and insecurities creep in, making it hard to build a lasting connection. Trust means believing that your partner has your best interests at heart, will be there for you, and will remain honest and faithful. When I dive into the topic of trust, I'm speaking from a place of personal experience. There was a chapter in our marriage when betrayal reared its ugly head, and let me tell you, it stung. The pain ran so deep that divorce seemed like a plausible conversation. I couldn't fathom overcoming this. It was a betrayal that cut to the core, leaving a gaping hole of mistrust. In that moment, I was lost, unsure of how to navigate the path ahead. In relationships, trust is like the sturdy foundation that holds everything together. Whether you're starting a marriage, navigating the ups and downs of a long-term commitment, or dreaming of a future together, trust is what makes your connection strong and lasting. Trust isn't just a feeling that comes and goes; it's the solid ground of security, respect, and understanding. It's not just about not doubting your partner, but it's about believing in their honesty, reliability, and loyalty. In a world full of uncertainties that can make relationships shaky, making sure trust is strong and keeping it that way becomes a promise you make to each other. Trust extends beyond fidelity; it encompasses reliability, honesty, and consistency. It's the foundation upon which partners feel safe, respected, and valued. Building and preserving this pillar requires a commitment to transparency, consistency, and integrity. Trust isn't a milestone but a journey—an ongoing process of building, nurturing, and safeguarding. It's not built overnight but through consistent actions, honest communication, and empathetic understanding. It's like planting a seed and nurturing it into a strong tree. Each honest conversation, kept promise, and supportive action helps that tree grow stronger. We had none of this at the time. How could I trust him again?

Actions speak volumes in the language of trust. Consistency between words and actions, honoring commitments, and being dependable forms the framework upon which trust is built. In the discord of daily life, nurturing trust involves actively demonstrating reliability and honesty. To be candid, this was a difficult phase for me. I was committed to every step needed to rebuild our foundation, but I struggled to trust him. Was he where he said he was? Did he tell the whole truth or leave pieces out? There were movies and songs that took me back to that dark uncomfortable, hurtful place. How do I get past these thoughts and triggers? Thinking about the effective communication that I had worked on, I had to open up. I had to tell him my struggles on the inside.

Trusting that your vulnerabilities will be met with love, support, and understanding enhances the depth and authenticity of your connection. In the process of rewriting your love story, trust is nurtured through consistent actions and behaviors that align with honesty, reliability, and integrity. It is built over time through small gestures, acts of kindness, and keeping the promises you make to one another. Trust is not given blindly but earned through a series of consistent actions and demonstrations of commitment. Remember, trust is a delicate and precious element that requires effort, communication, and patience to cultivate and maintain. It takes time to rebuild and strengthen, but its rewards are immeasurable. I learned to talk it out. I had to get vulnerability with myself and God. I needed his strength to get through this. Then, I had to get vulnerable with my husband. I'm so thankful that God hears our prayers. I was hesitant to have the discussion of trust with my husband, but he actually raised the topic. I remember so vividly that he mentioned how he was going to do whatever it took to gain my trust back. He would call often when he was out, update me if things changed, and communicate more. He was trying and it showed. It gave me assurance that we were in this together. Vulnerability becomes the bridge that strengthens the foundation of trust. It's the willingness to expose one's fears, dreams, and uncertainties, forging a path towards emotional intimacy. In relationships, being open and honest about your feelings helps you feel closer to each other and understand each other better. It's about recognizing and validating each other's emotions, nurturing an environment where both partners feel heard, understood, and supported. Vulnerability is about being open and honest, even when it feels uncomfortable. It's showing your true self without fear of judgment. Being vulnerable means sharing your weaknesses, fears, and mistakes, and trusting your partner to accept you as you are.

Intimacy is more than just being physically close; it's about connecting emotionally, mentally, and spiritually. It's like sharing your dreams, fears, happiness, and vulnerabilities with someone. In today's world, where it's easy to get distracted, building intimacy is key to having a happy relationship. Real intimacy isn't just about being physically close; it's about having a deep emotional bond, trust, and being true to yourself. It's about feeling completely accepted and understood by your partner. It's creating a safe space where both of you can be yourselves without worrying about being judged or turned away. Emotional intimacy means being open and honest about your feelings, sharing your fears, hopes, and doubts without holding back. It's about creating a space where you can have deep talks and when your words really mean something. Even silence can say a lot. To build emotional intimacy, you need to listen carefully, understand each other, and be brave enough to speak your mind. It's about making a safe place where both of you feel heard, understood, and loved for being yourselves.

You might think you're close to someone just because you're physically close, but that's not always true intimacy. Take a moment to think about that. Can you really be close to your partner even if you're not touching? It's an interesting idea to consider. You see, intimacy in relationships doesn't always come from physical contact. Every couple finds their own ways to feel close that don't rely on just being physical. Here are a few to consider:

1. **Emotional Connection:** Engage in deep and meaningful conversations that explore each other's thoughts, feelings, and dreams. Share your vulnerabilities, fears, and

aspirations, allowing yourselves to be fully seen and understood by one another.

____

____

____

2. **Quality Time:** Dedicate uninterrupted time to be together, engaging in activities that you both enjoy. This can include going for walks, cooking together, having date nights, or simply cuddling on the couch. The focus should be on creating shared experiences and building a strong bond.

____

____

____

3. **Physical Affection:** Physical touch plays a vital role in nurturing intimacy. Show affection through hugs, kisses, holding hands, and gentle touches. Take the time to be present with each other physically and explore intimate moments that bring you closer together.

____

____

4. **Shared Adventures:** Seek out new experiences and adventures as a couple. This could involve traveling, trying new hobbies, or participating in activities that challenge

and excite you both. Sharing novel experiences can deepen your connection and create lasting memories.

____

____

____

5. **Open and Honest Communication:** Establish a safe space for open and honest communication. Encourage each other to express desires, needs, and concerns without fear of judgment. Active listening, empathy, and understanding are crucial in fostering intimacy through communication.

____

____

____

6. **Mutual Support:** Be each other's cheerleaders and pillars of support. Show genuine interest and offer encouragement in each other's goals, dreams, and aspirations. Celebrate achievements together and provide comfort during challenging times.

____

____

7. **Intimacy Beyond the Physical:** Intimacy extends beyond physical closeness. Explore other forms of connection, such as intellectual intimacy through engaging in

stimulating conversations or spiritual intimacy through shared beliefs and practices.

____

____

____

8. **Trust and Vulnerability:** Cultivate an environment of trust, where both partners feel safe to be vulnerable with one another. Honesty, reliability, and confidentiality are essential components of building trust, allowing for deeper emotional intimacy.

____

____

____

9. **Appreciation and Gratitude:** Express appreciation and gratitude for one another regularly. Acknowledge and celebrate the unique qualities and contributions each partner brings to the relationship. This fosters a sense of validation and strengthens the emotional bond.

____

____

____

10. **Intimacy Rituals:** Establish rituals that are meaningful to both of you. It could be a weekly date night, a daily check-in, or a shared bedtime routine. These rituals create a sense

of predictability, stability, and connection within your relationship.

____
____
____

Remember, intimacy is a dynamic and evolving aspect of a relationship. It requires ongoing effort, nurturing, and adaptability to meet the changing needs of both partners. By prioritizing and investing in intimacy, you can create a deeper and more fulfilling connection in your relationship.

There was a phase in my marriage where intimacy, on every level, vanished. Trust went out the window, and communication was on life support. We were hurtling down a destructive path at breakneck speed, heading straight for divorce. Our friendship, once a pillar, seemed a distant memory. Every attempt at conversation turned into a battleground. It was tough. So tough that communicating with my husband required resorting to writing letters. Wrap your head around that—we shared a home, a bed, yet the only way I could reach him was through written words. These were desperate times, a make-or-break moment in our marriage. We knew we had to take action. Both of us acknowledged that our upbringing lacked a model of a healthy, robust relationship, and we were determined to create something different for our children, for our own lives. So, we made a pact to do the work. We sat down, had a heart-to-heart conversation, and decided to embark on this journey, fully aware that it would be painful. Tears would flow, anger would surface, and sadness would linger. It was going to dredge up emotions I had tried to bury. But we understood the necessity of facing it head-on. The work had to be done. It's a peculiar realization, not exactly hilarious, but intriguing nonetheless—discovering that I couldn't be intimate with my husband until I embraced intimacy with myself. I had to go on a date with myself, get to know the ins and outs of who I was. But here's the kicker: I couldn't truly be intimate with myself until I fostered an intimate connection with God. That, my friend, is the cornerstone of your first intimate relationship.

Here's a truth bomb: without intimacy with God, you're missing out on intimacy in every relationship, including the one with yourself. I had a history with God—I'd witnessed his glory, basked in his favor. But there was a distance, a gap between us. I was grappling with emotions, feeling angry, and not really comprehending what was happening or why I felt the way I did. Instead of seeking Him during these moments of confusion, I took a step back, withdrew. Little did I know that act of withdrawal turned out to be more painful than anything else.

Stepping back to reconnect with God was a game-changer for me. It was the key to unlocking intimacy with myself, paving the way for a deeper connection with my husband. In the realm of spiritual intimacy, it takes three: me, my husband, and God. Nurturing that spiritual connection is crucial because let's face it—maintaining a marriage or a long-term relationship is no walk in the park. It's like blending two distinct stories, two different perspectives, upbringings, examples, and life experiences into one. Achieving unity is a tough job. But here's the secret sauce: God at the center. Having Him there reveals the areas of our relationship that need work. A spiritual connection allows me to pray for my husband, pray with him, and have him pray for me—a sacred trifecta that keeps us grounded.

There were days when I couldn't muster the words in prayer for myself, and that's when I knew my husband had my back in the prayer department. Our journey to where we are today wasn't always a smooth ride, but one thing we've learned is the power of prayer and priorities. God comes first, followed by my husband, the head of our home. Trusting my husband didn't happen overnight. I had my doubts, questioned if we'd make it. It led me to revisit the root of it all—a lack of intimacy with God. Only by nurturing that intimacy could I reconnect with myself and, in turn, deepen the bond with my spouse.

Creating a vulnerable space was my starting point to pinpoint the areas of my life that needed attention. Now, my husband, like many men, wasn't well-versed in vulnerability. From a young age, the narrative was clear: "Boys don't cry. Stop those tears. Be a man." It's a societal script that most men grow up hearing. So, we had some serious work to do. It took time, but I eventually saw my husband through a different lens. We delved into those tough conversations, and as a result, I began to witness him as the man God intended him to be, shedding the image of the one who had caused me pain in the past. The lens shifted—I no longer saw the hurt he brought me; I saw the strength he was providing today. It wasn't a quick fix; it took effort, time, and there was no set schedule. We navigated this journey day by day, sometimes even hour by hour. We prayed, shed tears, had heart-to-hearts, shared laughs, and revisited memories. Anger and sadness were part of the mix—all these emotions were like building blocks leading us to where we stand today. Focusing on rebuilding intimacy became a crucial part of reclaiming trust, reinforcing the belief that he has transformed into the man God intended him to be.

He had to go through a growth process, and that was a lesson I needed to grasp. Understanding that he wasn't the same man I married was a crucial realization. When I said, "I do," it encompassed the man he was then and the man standing before me today. The real challenge lies in weathering the storms within marriages and relationships because that's where you see the fruits of your labor. There's a purpose behind the challenges we face, a reason for the trials. Back then, I didn't get it—I was even angry at God. Now, I see the wisdom in the path He led me down. My message to you today is this: you can break free from being stuck.

Healing your marriage or relationship is entirely possible, but it's a team effort— it takes two. The journey kicks off with your willingness, and then you layer on vulnerability. Engage in those tough conversations about the intimacy gaps, the trust issues, and the barriers in communication. Dive into the intricacies of love languages. What makes your partner feel loved? Is it through gifts, quality time, or physical touch? Understanding both your own and your significant other's love language is pivotal. It's the key to unlocking the door that leads to genuine connection with your partner. Moving beyond the surface requires effort and courage, but the rewards are immeasurable. By building trust, fostering intimacy, and embracing vulnerability, you can create a connection that is truly unbreakable.

Remember, this journey is ongoing. Keep nurturing trust, seeking intimacy, and embracing vulnerability. As you continue to move beyond the surface, you'll find that your relationship becomes richer and more fulfilling.

TAKE ACTION:

1. How does embracing vulnerability and opening up about your deepest fears and insecurities strengthen the bonds of trust and intimacy within your relationship, paving the way for a more authentic and fulfilling love story?

   ____
   ____
   ____

2. In what ways can exploring the layers beneath the surface of your emotions and experiences lead to a deeper understanding of yourself and your partner, fostering a sense of connection and empathy that transcends superficial interactions in your journey to rewrite your love story?

   ____
   ____
   ____

Notes:

Notes:

CHAPTER FIVE

BUILDING on a SOLID FOUNDATION

Just like building a house, creating a lasting and fulfilling relationship requires a solid foundation. A solid foundation in a relationship means having shared values, mutual respect, and a deep understanding of each other. It's about creating a partnership that can withstand challenges and grow stronger over time. Without a solid foundation, relationships can easily crumble when faced with difficulties. Think of your relationship as a building. If the foundation is weak, the building can collapse. But if it's strong, it can stand tall and weather any storm.

Now that we have all of the tools, we are able to start laying the groundwork for a love story that stands the test of time. It's about consciously tending to the soil upon which your relationship grows, nurturing it with trust, watering it with communication, and allowing the sunshine of mutual respect to illuminate its path. We've all heard the tale from the Bible about the perils of building on sand versus a rock, with the rock symbolizing God's unwavering strength. (Matthew 7:24-27) When the concept of rebuilding on a solid foundation crosses my mind, I'm drawn to the Book of Nehemiah. If you haven't delved into Nehemiah's journey, I highly recommend it. Nehemiah harbored a powerful vision centered around rebuilding. The time had come to reconstruct the walls, as beautifully chronicled in the Book of Nehemiah.

The book of Nehemiah offers valuable lessons that can be applied to rebuilding a relationship on a solid foundation. Just as Nehemiah began his mission by acknowledging the problem and praying for guidance, rebuilding a relationship starts with recognizing the issues and seeking wisdom, whether through prayer, reflection, or open communication. Nehemiah meticulously planned the rebuilding process, understanding the scope of work and resources needed. Similarly, restoring a relationship requires careful consideration of the steps needed to heal and strengthen the bond, including setting clear goals and intentions. Nehemiah encountered significant opposition but remained steadfast. In relationships, challenges and external pressures will arise, but staying committed and resilient is crucial to rebuilding and maintaining a strong connection.

It all began with a vision—my vision was to transform my marriage into the best it could ever be. Crafting a solid foundation in a relationship is like laying the groundwork for long-term success and happiness. It's not a one-time thing; it demands consistent effort and adaptability. Relationships are dynamic, ever-changing, and embracing growth, change, and shared learning is key. Keep the commitment alive by dedicating time, energy, and love to your relationship. Building a solid foundation is an ongoing adventure, demanding mutual commitment, patience, and a deep understanding of each other.

I envision my marriage as an inspiration of hope, a living example that other couples can conquer their challenges. It's not just a personal triumph; it's a legacy I want to leave for my daughters—a standard they should aspire to. Building this exemplary marriage starts with a strong foundation. So, how do you lay the groundwork? It involves discussions on trust, accountability, and communication. It extends beyond the physical, embracing emotional, intellectual, and spiritual intimacy. These elements collectively form the bedrock of the foundation you need to construct within your relationship. Shift your focus to the positive and carve out quality time, even amidst chaos of life like children, jobs, and other responsibilities. It might involve a cozy movie night after the kids are in bed, a lunch date if your schedule allows, or a morning breakfast ritual before diving into the day. The key is getting creative to prioritize what truly matters. Staying connected is vital—whether it's through text messages, FaceTime, or any means that keeps the bond intact. Consider establishing a routine, like sending a morning text every Monday, to keep the connection alive, especially if your spouse leaves earlier than you do.

If our mornings don't allow for a heart-to-heart, a quick text becomes my way of saying, "Hey, I'm thinking of you, hoping your day is fantastic." It's those little gestures that matter. Navigate household responsibilities by finding a compromise that works for both of you. If my spouse is pulling a late work shift and the laundry needs attention, I toss in a load. Marriage isn't always a neat 50/50 division; sometimes it's a dance of 90/10, 60/40, or 70/30. It's about understanding each other's needs and stepping in, even when the balance isn't perfectly equal.

Constructing a solid foundation demands effort, and it's a far cry from the traditional notion of the wife staying home. We've moved beyond those old-fashioned roles. In our dynamic, both of us contribute to making money, both of us handle household chores, and both of us play a role in nurturing and tending to our children. It's not a one-sided affair; it's a tag team effort, a partnership where we share responsibilities and work together to build something meaningful.

In the days of my girls' youth, he'd tackle hair combing duties, giving me a breather. Our bedtime routine was a tag team effort—one night it was me, the next it was him. Every household is unique; find what suits yours. The crucial part is that it's a joint effort. Take a moment to redefine your relationship goals and hash them out with your significant other. Assess whether your current path aligns with both your individual and shared aspirations. And remember, it's perfectly fine if the balance isn't 50/50 every day; some days, it might sway more towards 70/30, and that's okay.

Balance is key; one day you might bear the heavy load, and the next, it could be his turn. It's about understanding that you both contribute to constructing that foundation. Break free from the routine and venture into new experiences as a couple. Shake things up with novel activities, explore uncharted places, or embark on shared adventures. Injecting this freshness can infuse excitement and renewed energy into the relationship. Whether it's trying a new restaurant, reading a book together, sharing a devotion, attending a concert, or exploring a new city or bed and breakfast—go ahead, try something different.

Your significant other, your life partner, is more than just a lover—they should be your ultimate confidant and best friend. It's a relationship where you can share love, but also confide, pray, and uplift each other. Together, you weather the rough days, offering a listening ear and a supportive hand to pull each other out of the lows. Cultivate intimacy and emotional connection by indulging in quality time, physical affection, and deep conversations. Reignite the spark and make it a priority to nurture the emotional bond that forms the foundation of your partnership.

Embarking on this journey together requires building a foundation, focusing on the positive, and looking ahead, not dwelling on the past. Prioritize the future and dedicate quality time to your significant other because what matters to them deserves time. It's the little things that count, where understanding your spouse's love language plays a key role. Whether it's a cozy movie night or a thoughtful conversation over dinner with a glass of wine, the gestures speak volumes. Establishing trust may be challenging based on your history, but it's crucial for both to move in the right direction.

Engage in open communication, especially when discussing finances. Be honest about your current situation and work together to create a plan that aligns with your shared goals.

Remember, it's not just about the present or the children; it's about building a future together.

Envision a life where, once the kids have grown and flown the nest, it's still the two of you. Strengthening your relationship requires a commitment to each other and the foundation you've built together.

Embark on the journey of rebuilding, a crucial time to lay the foundation anew. Reflect on the elements that were missing in your marriage or relationship and consider integrating them to foster growth. Understand that the path ahead won't be effortless, acknowledging imperfections on both sides. Maintain an open and transparent dialogue, ensuring honesty in your conversations. Approach discussions with a calm demeanor, choosing words carefully to avoid unnecessary hurt. Remember, rebuilding requires patience, understanding, and a commitment to creating a stronger foundation.

Take a thoughtful approach to your conversations, considering the impact of your words before expressing them. Engage in an evening dialogue with your partner, expressing how certain statements made you feel throughout the day. Recognize that misunderstandings are common, and if your spouse cares about you, they will clarify their intentions and apologize if necessary. Foster an open dialogue that allows both of you to communicate openly, dedicating time to rebuild trust and establish the foundation your relationship deserves. Prioritize elements such as trust, transparency, and accountability during this pivotal rebuilding phase. Embrace accountability as a powerful tool for establishing healthy boundaries and effective communication. Clearly articulate your expectations and desires while respecting your significant other's boundaries, fostering a balanced and secure environment for mutual growth.

Recognize the imperfections in both you and your spouse, emphasizing positive aspects.

Now, as you embark on rebuilding, you lay the foundation for a new chapter in your love story. This pivotal moment defines the trajectory of your future relationship, marking the beginning of a rewritten narrative. It's time to start building anew.

TAKE ACTION:

1. What steps can you take to identify and strengthen the weak spots in your relationship's foundation, ensuring that it's built on a solid framework of trust, communication, and shared values as you embark on rewriting your love story?

---

2. How can you navigate the complexities of laying a solid foundation in your relationship, considering factors such as past experiences, individual differences, and external pressures, to create a strong and resilient base for your shared journey of growth and transformation in rewriting your love story?

Notes:

CHAPTER
SIX

BOUNDARIES and BRIDGES

Now, it is time to focus on the importance of setting boundaries in your relationship. Boundaries might sound like barriers, but in reality, they are bridges that connect you and your partner in a healthy, respectful, and loving way. Boundaries are the limits you set in your relationship to protect your well-being and maintain mutual respect. They define what you are comfortable with and how you want to be treated. Think of boundaries as the rules of your personal space—emotional, physical, and mental.

Creating boundaries doesn't mean pushing your partner away; it means valuing yourself and keeping your own identity strong in your relationship. Whether you're getting married, sticking it out in a long-term relationship, or just imagining your future with someone, having clear boundaries helps keep your relationship healthy and happy. Setting boundaries isn't about putting up walls to keep your partner out; it's about building bridges to better understand each other. Boundaries show where you stop and your partner starts, making sure both of you are respected as individuals with your own needs, values, and identities. In a world where relationships can sometimes make it hard to tell where you end and your partner begins, setting boundaries is a way to take care of yourself and show respect for each other.

Boundaries cover your feelings, personal space, and thoughts. They show what's okay and what's not okay in your relationship, making sure you feel safe, respected, and heard. It's really important to set and talk about these boundaries because they're a big part of keeping your relationship healthy and fair for both of you. Respect is like the glue that keeps boundaries strong. It means listening to your partner's rules, understanding why they're important, and not crossing them. It's also about being open to change and understanding that boundaries can shift as your relationship grows. Respecting each other's boundaries doesn't mean pulling away from each other; it actually brings you closer. It shows that you respect each other's independence and care about building a relationship based on treating each other right.

Creating strong boundaries in a relationship isn't just a one-time thing; it's an ongoing talk you have with your partner. It's about figuring out how to deal with all the feelings, needs, and changes that come up. It's finding the right balance where you both feel like individuals but also like you're part of a team. It's a place where respect and love can grow, even when you have clear lines drawn. So, whether you're getting married, working through years together, or thinking about what's next, setting and respecting boundaries is key to your love story. It's like going on a journey together, knowing that boundaries in love don't push you apart but actually show you the way to a stronger relationship, where you both understand each other better and treat each other right.

I've identified a few types of boundaries to consider and how to set them when recreating your newfound. relationship:

TYPES OF BOUNDARIES:

1. **Emotional Boundaries**: These involve your feelings and emotional needs. Emotional boundaries protect your heart and mind. They include things like how you want to be treated emotionally, how much emotional energy you can give, and how you handle emotional conflicts.

____

____

2. **Physical Boundaries**: These relate to your personal space and physical needs. Physical boundaries include things like personal space, physical affection, and privacy.

____

____

____

3. **Mental Boundaries**: These involve your thoughts, opinions, and beliefs. Mental boundaries respect each other's viewpoints and intellectual space. They include things like respecting each other's opinions, allowing each other to have independent thoughts, and not trying to control each other's beliefs.

____

____

____

HOW TO SET BOUNDARIES:

1. **Time Boundaries**: These involve how you allocate your time. Time boundaries help you balance your time between your relationship, work, hobbies, and personal time.

____

2. **Know Your Limits**: Before you can set boundaries, you need to understand your own limits. Reflect on what makes you feel comfortable and what doesn't. Consider your emotional, physical, mental, and time needs.

3. **Communicate Clearly**: Once you know your boundaries, communicate them clearly to your partner. Use "I" statements to express your needs without blaming or accusing. For example, "I need some alone time after work to relax" is clearer and less confrontational than "You always bother me when I get home."

4. **Be Consistent**: Consistency is key to maintaining boundaries. Once you've set a boundary, stick to it. This shows your partner that you're serious about your needs and helps reinforce the importance of respecting each other's limits.

____

____

5. **Respect Your Partner's Boundaries**: Just as you set your own boundaries, respect your partner's. Listen to their needs and make an effort to honor them. This mutual respect creates a balanced and healthy relationship.

   ____

   ____

   ____

6. **Revisit and Adjust**: Boundaries aren't set in stone. As your relationship evolves, so might your needs. Regularly check in with each other to discuss and adjust your boundaries as needed.

   ____

   ____

   ____

Congratulations on reaching this positive place in your journey. As you've navigated through the work, shed tears, and experienced healing, it's crucial to maintain this newfound harmony with your significant other. Building a solid foundation is just the beginning; now, it's time to set and reinforce boundaries. Communicate your needs and expectations openly, ensuring that both partners feel valued and heard. Consider aspects like personal space, communication, time commitments, and emotional well-being when defining these crucial boundaries.

Now that you've pinpointed your needs, it's time to carve out your boundaries with clarity. Specify which behaviors, actions, or situations align with your comfort zone and which ones don't. This isn't about placing blame or criticizing your significant other; it's about honing in on your feelings and needs. Define the consequences when boundaries are overlooked, emphasizing their significance and fostering accountability. Remember, boundaries operate in both directions. Display the same respect for your partner's boundaries as you anticipate for your own. It's a mutual understanding that ensures a balanced and considerate relationship.

Take charge of your energy, your surroundings, and the company you keep. Setting boundaries is key. Both you and your partner must establish clear limits, guiding your actions and decisions.

Cultivate a space where your relationship can flourish. Weed out any negativity—be it friends, couples, or family members—telling you it won't work or it's over. You've put in the effort, identified your desires and needs. Now, it's crucial to enforce those boundaries. You're on the path to what you want; make sure nothing derails your journey.

Navigate the challenges of communication in your marriage or relationship by crafting thoughtful boundaries. You don't need to be a lawyer; just initiate open conversations. Sit your partner down and inquire about their feelings, seeking clarity with questions like, "I felt this way, could you elaborate?" Communication is key. Set boundaries to ensure you don't let issues fester. Make a pact: no going to bed angry. If unresolved emotions lingered in your past, create a boundary to address them promptly. Declare that in this relationship, going to bed upset is a no-go. Foster an environment where discussing feelings is the norm, not an exception.

Protect your journey of rebuilding and making things right with a shield of caution. Pay attention to negative influences among your family and friends, especially those who don't truly support your efforts. While it can feel good to vent, be careful who you share it with. Avoid people who just make you feel worse or spread your private issues online. Your personal space is important, so don't let toxic people invade it. Feeling upset with your partner doesn't always mean it's over. Be cautious of friends who quickly tell you to leave. Keep your private matters private. The less you tell the wrong people, the safer your relationship will be. When it comes to setting boundaries, it's like doing some spring cleaning—getting rid of the negative energy. Not everyone is happy about seeing you and your spouse working things out. Some people thrive on others' problems. If you have unsupportive or discouraging people around who aren't helping you both stay strong and work through things, it might be time to say goodbye to them. Letting go isn't easy, but it's important for moving forward. You're growing and moving up, and sometimes that means leaving certain people and things behind. Going through this journey with your spouse means sticking together, even if not everyone is cheering you on. Through it all, my advice is to stay consistent. Consistency is your best friend on this uphill climb.

Whether it's movie night every Friday or breakfast outings every Saturday, the key is to make your own rhythm and stick to it. Your formula for connection is your business, but the magic lies in consistency. Keep the flame alive with regularity in your actions, conversations, and communication. Guard against the old habits sneaking back in—avoid the pitfalls of communication lapses, excessive busyness, work overshadowing, or kids taking priority. The name of the game is consistency; it's the glue that holds the special moments and shared commitments together.

Open up those lines of communication! I used to nudge my husband, saying, "We need to catch up; work's been a whirlwind. What's on your agenda for the evening? Any plans for the weekend?" Quality time doesn't demand breaking the bank or jet-setting; it's about connection. Whether it's a cozy night at home, a bubble bath, a glass of wine, cooking together, watching a movie, or indulging in massages, get creative. The key is not just creativity but consistency.

Keep the flame burning with regular moments of togetherness. Resist the pull of stagnation; don't let the old version of you creep back in. It's about evolving and staying committed to that growth.

Don't allow those outdated negative thoughts and feedback to stage a comeback. It's crucial to recognize them, be self-aware, and shut them down before they gain momentum. This is where boundaries come into play—setting a firm line against the negativity. Stay consistent in your commitment to positivity and growth. Moreover, leave space for the evolving versions of you and your significant other. Embrace the change, make room for the ongoing journey of growth, and let the old narratives fade away.

Prepare for the person you're with today to evolve over the next five years. The aim is shared growth, a journey you both embark on together. Embrace change; it's not always a negative force. Fear of the unknown might make us reluctant, but I urge you to welcome what lies ahead. Create space for positive shifts in your relationship. Be open to trying new things, breaking the routine. Perhaps new friends and couples will enter your space, bringing challenges that foster growth and fresh perspectives. Acknowledge that you're on the right path, having put in the work and committed to doing more. But remember, you must make room for what's yet to come on this exciting journey.

The person you said "I do" to—whether it was years, a year, or just recently—is bound to evolve. Change is inevitable, but here's the magic: as long as both of you keep growing, stay consistent, keep the faith alive, stay focused, radiate positivity, and engage in open communication, it's a recipe for success. Take accountability, reflect on your current state, and envision where you want to be. It's not just a shot in the dark; it's a surefire way to make it work. But here's the kicker: you've got to be a gatekeeper, fiercely guarding the essence of what makes your connection special. Set those boundaries, sharp and clear. If something from the past didn't vibe with your marriage and threatens your future, shut it down quick. Creating boundaries ensures both of you are on the same page about where you stand and where you're headed. Guard your relationship like a sacred treasure—be the gatekeeper. There's no room for anyone or anything trying to break or hinder it. It's sacred; treat it as such.

Maintain those boundaries, stay consistent, and remember, taking it day by day or even hour by hour is perfectly okay. The decision to spend your life with someone is realistic, but let's be honest, sometimes they might annoy you. It doesn't mean you don't love them; it's just part of the journey.

Sure, things might be said or done that ruffle your feathers, leaving you a bit bothered. Yet, when the dust settles, you realize this is the person you've chosen to navigate the journey of a lifetime with. Rebuilding and uniting for a brighter future don't mean it's a drama-free zone. Let's keep it real; life throws curveballs. In my own journey with my husband, I've learned that wanting to spend your life with someone doesn't exempt you from occasional turbulence. We face it daily, but what keeps me going is the certainty that I want him by my side. I've witnessed the transformation—he's not the man I married almost 18 years ago, and the love we share today is a testament to the growth we've experienced together.

Let's keep it real—it's crucial to be grounded in reality. You're human, your spouse is human, and guess what? That's perfectly okay. Embrace your humanity as you navigate this journey together. Cut each other some slack. If your spouse's message didn't land as intended, offer some grace, throw in a few questions for clarification. What did you mean by that? Is this what you intended? Communication is a dance, and sometimes the steps get a bit tangled.

Sure, there will be ups and downs, disagreements, and the occasional clash of ideas—especially with kids, dreams, and plans in the mix. It's part of the package. Bumping heads is part of the course, but as long as you both know that, at the end of the day, you're committed to spending your lives together, you can navigate through it. Be the gatekeeper of your love, extend that grace, set those boundaries, stay consistent, and make room for the beautiful surprises ahead. You've put in the work, unpacked your hearts, and now you're in the process of rewriting your unique love story.

TAKE ACTION:

1. How can you navigate the delicate balance between setting boundaries to protect yourself while still remaining open and connected in your relationship, ensuring that boundaries serve as bridges to deeper understanding rather than barriers to intimacy?

____

____

____

2. In what ways can you identify and communicate your boundaries effectively, recognizing that they are not walls to keep others out but pathways to mutual respect and growth in your love story?

____

____

____

Notes:

Notes:

CHAPTER SEVEN

OPENING a NEW CHAPTER

After working on the foundation of your relationship, setting boundaries, and building trust and intimacy, it's time to reignite the spark and explore new horizons together. Rediscovery and adventure can breathe new life into your relationship, making it more vibrant and fulfilling.

Rediscovery is about finding new aspects of your partner and your relationship. Over time, it's easy to fall into routines and take each other for granted. Rediscovery helps you reconnect and see each other with fresh eyes. It's like turning the page to a new chapter in your love story, filled with excitement and curiosity. As time goes by, both partners change, dreams change, and the way we see things changes. Rediscovering each other in a relationship means seeing these changes as chances to grow instead of problems. It's about giving each other room to grow while still keeping our connection strong. Rediscovery means having conversations that uncover new things we're excited about, dreams we have, and things we want to do, making a space where both partners feel encouraged to grow.

Rediscovering each other involves peeling back the layers to uncover hidden depths. It's about nurturing curiosity, exploring shared interests, and actively engaging in moments that foster connection. Rediscovery isn't solely about learning something new; it's also about rekindling the familiarity that brought two souls together. It's about celebrating the essence of your partner—their quirks, their evolving ambitions, and the core of their being. Rediscovery breathes new life into intimacy and connection. It's about exploring new aspects of physical closeness and emotional depth. Rediscovering intimacy involves open communication about desires, fears, and aspirations, reigniting the spark that first ignited the flames of love. It's about creating opportunities for shared experiences, nurturing an environment where both partners feel seen, heard, and understood in their growth.

Rediscovering each other isn't like a trip with a set endpoint; it's more like an ongoing adventure. It's about changing, growing, and getting to know each other again as life keeps changing. Rediscovery is like a compass guiding your love story. It's about welcoming change, helping each other grow, and seeing your relationship in a new way with open hearts and fresh eyes.

Adventure adds excitement and novelty to your relationship. It's about stepping out of your comfort zone and experiencing new things together. Having adventures in relationships goes beyond just exciting trips; it's more about having a certain mindset—a way of thinking that's open to spontaneity, curiosity, and exploring things together. It's also about finding happiness in everyday moments, learning new things about each other, and making sure both partners feel excited and involved. Bringing adventure into a relationship means finding fun in everyday life. It's about being spontaneous—doing surprises for each other, trying new things together, and breaking away from your usual routine. It's as simple as trying new recipes together, embarking on impromptu road trips, or exploring hobbies that ignite a sense of excitement. Adventure blooms in the moments where you abandon the familiar and embrace the unknown together. Engaging in shared adventures creates opportunities for bonding, communication, and understanding.

The challenges faced during adventures become opportunities for teamwork, problem-solving, and building trust. It's about celebrating successes, learning from failures, and growing together through shared experiences.

TAKE ACTION:

1. How can you redefine the concept of adventure in your relationship to include not just grand gestures, but also the beauty found in the everyday moments of connection and discovery?

____

____

____

2. In what ways can you approach the process of rediscovery as an ongoing journey of exploration and growth, embracing change and spontaneity to keep your love story vibrant and alive?

____

____

____

Notes:

Notes:

Conclusion

Congratulations on completing the journey of "Unpack Your Heart"! You've embarked on a transformative voyage to rewrite your love story, and along the way, you've explored essential steps to enriching your relationship.

First, you learned about the power of willingness - the openness to change and growth within yourself and your partnership. You discovered the strength that comes from prayer, seeking guidance and support from God as you navigate the ups and downs of love.

Accountability became a cornerstone of your journey, as you took responsibility for your actions and emotions, fostering trust and honesty in your relationship. Effective communication became your ally, helping you bridge gaps, resolve conflicts, and deepen your connection with your partner. Through the journey of forgiveness, you embraced the healing balm that soothes wounds and allows for renewal, paving the way for trust to blossom. You recognized that trust is the bedrock of your relationship, providing security, respect, and understanding. Intimacy and vulnerability became your guiding lights, as you opened your hearts to each other, fostering a deep sense of connection and empathy. You built a solid foundation for your love story, rooted in shared values, mutual respect, and support.

Setting boundaries became essential, ensuring that both partners felt safe, respected, and understood in the relationship. You embarked on a journey of rediscovery, embracing change and growth together, and infusing your relationship with adventure and spontaneity. As you close this chapter of your love story, remember that rewriting your love story is not a one-time event but an ongoing journey. It's about continually unpacking your heart, being willing to learn and grow, and nurturing your connection with your partner every step of the way.

Rewriting your love story is an ever-evolving process. Just as you have navigated through willingness and prayer, accountability and communication, forgiveness, trust, intimacy, vulnerability, building a solid foundation, setting boundaries, and rediscovery, you must continue to revisit these steps. Each stage of life and each new challenge will call you to unpack your heart anew. This is not a sign of weakness but of strength and commitment to love.

Keep in mind that honesty and openness are the threads that weave through each of the steps you've taken. By remaining transparent and truthful with yourself and your partner, you create a space where love can thrive. Don't shy away from difficult conversations; they are often the ones that bring the most growth and understanding.

Your relationship is a living, breathing entity that requires constant care and attention. Nurture it by prioritizing quality time, showing appreciation, and continuing to dream and plan together. Let your love story be one of mutual growth and shared joy, where both partners feel valued and heard. Vulnerability is where true connection happens. It's about showing up as your true self, flaws and all, and being accepted and loved for who you are. Embrace vulnerability not as a weakness but as a strength that deepens your bond and fosters real intimacy.

In the journey of love, it's important to celebrate the small victories. Every step forward, every resolved conflict, and every moment of connection is a testament to your commitment and love.

Recognize and appreciate these moments, for they build the foundation of a lasting relationship.

The future holds endless possibilities for your love story. Keep an open heart and a willing spirit, ready to embrace whatever comes your way. Continue to grow together, dream together, and support each other through the ups and downs. Your love story is beautiful and made up of hope, trust, and adventure.

As you move forward, keep in mind the words of 1 Corinthians 13:7: "Love bears all things, believes all things, hopes all things, endures all things." Let this be your guide as you navigate the journey ahead.

May your love story continue to unfold with joy, passion, and authenticity, as you embrace the beauty of vulnerability, trust, and adventure together. Here's to a lifetime of love, growth, and endless possibilities. Your love story is unique, powerful, and entirely yours to write. May it be filled with joy, passion, and authenticity, as you continue to unpack your heart and embrace the beautiful journey of rewriting your love story.

Thank you for joining me on this journey. Now, go forth and create the love story you've always dreamed of. The best is yet to come.

About the Author

Introducing Rita Carter, an author, certified coach, and captivating speaker, known for her lifechanging approach to rewriting love stories. Rita is dedicated to helping women break through their barriers, unlock their full potential, and create fulfilling, harmonious relationships in both their personal and professional lives.

With over two decades of experience in Corporate America and as a certified behavioral analysis consultant, particularly in the DISC method, Rita brings a unique blend of corporate savvy and relationship expertise to her coaching. Her insightful guidance helps clients understand and navigate the complexities of human behavior, empowering them to tackle complex interpersonal situations with confidence and clarity.

As the Founder and CEO of Breakthrough LLC, home of her signature program, Love Unlocked. Rita is committed to helping individuals overcome obstacles and achieve their highest potential. Her practical business acumen, combined with a deep understanding of interpersonal dynamics, provides a holistic approach to personal and professional growth. Rita's journey is driven by a passion for guiding others toward transformational breakthroughs. With this passion, she understands the complexities of human connection and combines it with her empathetic and nonjudgmental approach which allows her to build trust and create a safe space for her clients.

Whether she's speaking on stage or working one-on-one with clients, Rita's authenticity, warmth, and commitment shines through. She is on a mission to inspire, uplift, and empower others, sharing her personal triumphs and professional expertise to help people flourish in every aspect of their lives. Rita holds a Bachelor's in Business Administration, a Master's in Management, several certificates from Moody Theological Seminary, a coaching certification, A DISC trainer and consultant. Rita lives in Michigan with her husband of nearly 18 years and their two daughters.

CONNECT WITH ME

To learn more about Rita's coaching and speaking services or to schedule a free discovery call, email us at Clientcare@breakthroughready.com.

Visit www.breakthroughready.com for your free relationship checklist and to sign-up for our Monday Motivation newsletter.

Social Media:

Facebook: https://www.facebook.com/BreakthroughwithRita
Instagram: https://www.instagram.com/breakthroughwithrita/
LinkedIn: linkedin.com/in/rita-carter

www.ingramcontent.com/pod-product-compliance
Lightning Source LLC
Chambersburg PA
CBHW040541170726
48295CB00012B/553

* 9 7 8 1 9 5 5 1 0 7 3 0 3 *